This book belongs to:

_____

Table of Contents

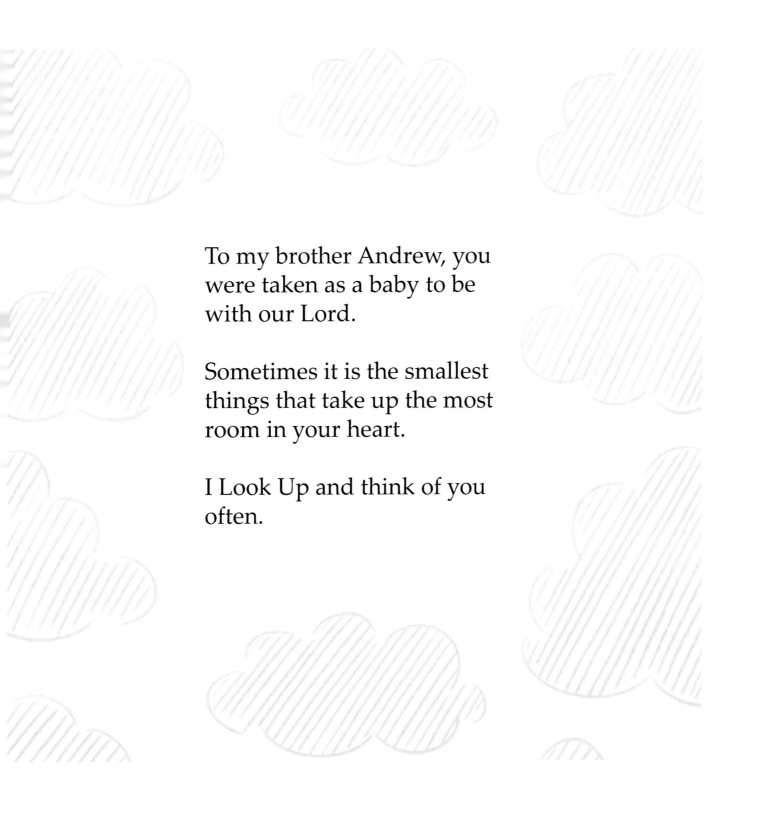

To my brother Andrew, you
were taken as a baby to be
with our Lord.

Sometimes it is the smallest
things that take up the most
room in your heart.

I Look Up and think of you
often.

"It was a gloomy, gloomy day."

Anna and her mom stood side by side at the cemetery. The funeral of Anna's dad had just finished and the people were leaving. As they walked away, they greeted Anna and her mom.

"Our sincere condolences," some said.
"We're sorry for your loss," said the others.

Mom nodded and thanked them while Anna stood next to her. Soon, they were the only ones left in the cemetery.

Anna and her mom looked nothing alike. Anna was a six-year-old girl with blond hair, blue eyes, and fair skin. Mom had dark hair, brown eyes, and a fair complexion. Everyone used to say that Anna looked just like her dad. The little girl loved her dad very much.

"Where's Daddy?" Anna asked. Mom sighed. She had been waiting for Anna to ask her that question ever since Dad died.

Mom knelt down in front of Anna and said, "Daddy is in Heaven now."

"Where is that?"
Anna asked.

"You see, when people die, they go to Heaven. Daddy has gone to Heaven. It's a beautiful place where good people find happiness," Mom explained.

"But I want to see Daddy," Anna said sadly.

Mom hugged the little girl and said, "I know you want to see him. I want that, too. But whenever you feel sad, all you have to do is look up. That's where Daddy is."

Then Mom stood up and took the little girl's hand.
Together, they went home.

The next morning, when Anna woke up, she looked out the window. In the backyard, she saw the princess castle that her dad built. She remembered how they used to play together.

"Good morning, Anna,"
Mom said.

The little girl turned around. Mom came into her room and walked toward her.

"I remember how you and your dad used to play in that castle."

"I miss him," Anna said.

Mom put her arm around Anna's shoulder and said, "I know. Just remember, when you think of Daddy, all you have to do is look up."

After breakfast, Anna went outside. She sat on the doorstep and looked at the garden. She remembered how Dad used to mow the lawn every Saturday while she played in the living room. Whenever she would hear the lawn mower, she would run to the window, and wave to Daddy.

With a sigh, the little girl looked up.

Then, she turned her head toward the garage. She remembered how she used to help Daddy wash the car sometimes. And whenever Mom would come home with groceries, Daddy would always come outside to help her bring the bags inside.

Each time Anna and her mom would step through the door, Daddy would bow down to them. That always made the little girl giggle.

Once again, she looked up. This time, she said, "I miss you, Daddy."

Being outside made Anna feel sad. So she stood up and went inside the house. Next to the door was a coat rack. Daddy's coat was still hanging on the rack. His favorite shoes were on the floor.

Anna looked up and closed
her eyes. When she did that,
she could see Daddy's smiling
face in her mind.

The little girl spent the rest of the day with Mom. They tried to do things that made them happy. When it was time for dinner, Mom opened the cupboard. She saw Dad's favorite cereal.

Anna watched as Mom bowed her head and covered her face with one hand. The little girl walked over and took Mom's hand.

Mom quickly wiped the tears from her eyes and faced the little girl.

"What is it, Anna?
Do you need
anything?"

""I know you're sad, Mom. You miss Daddy just like me.

But you told me that he is in Heaven now, a wonderful place where good people go," said the little girl.

Then she squeezed Mom's hand and said, "Whenever we miss Daddy, all we need to do is look up."

Things to Know About Heaven

Losing a loved one is a devastating thing.
For young children, it could make them feel sad, lost, and confused.
As a parent, you need to help your child cope. One way to do this is by putting their mind at ease. Telling your child how their loved one has gone to a beautiful place known as Heaven could make them feel less sad.
None of us really know what Heaven looks like. When you try to explain this to your child, use happy, positive words. Describe a nice place where your loved one will find happiness. A place where they don't feel pain or sadness.
Just like in this story, Mom helped Anna cope by telling her that her dad was happy in Heaven. And whenever your child wants to remember the person they lost, you can encourage them to "look up."

Beautiful Quotes About Heaven

Sometimes, explaining abstract concepts like Heaven and Hell can be easier by using quotes to introduce them. Here are some quotes about Heaven from the New International Version (Bible) that you can use when explaining Heaven to your child.

He will wipe every tear from their eyes. There will be no more death or mourning or crying or pain, for the old order of things has passed away. –Revelation 21:4

In my Father's house are many rooms; if it were not so, I would have told you. I am going there to prepare a place for you. –John 14:2

However, as it is written: "No eye has seen, no ear has heard, no mind has conceived what God has prepared for those who love him. –1 Corinthians 2:9

Jesus answered him, "Truly I tell you, today you will be with me in paradise." –Luke 23:43

Instead, they were longing for a better country—a heavenly one. Therefore God is not ashamed to be called their God, for he has prepared a city for them. –Hebrews 11:16

May your God go with you.

References
25 Bible verses about Heaven (NIV). (n.d.). ReformedWiki.
https://reformedwiki.com/verses/heaven/niv

Made in United States
Orlando, FL
26 February 2024

44115334R00024